Connected Mathematics™

Filling and Wrapping

Three-Dimensional Measurement

Student Edition

Glenda Lappan
James T. Fey
William M. Fitzgerald
Susan N. Friel
Elizabeth Difanis Phillips

PEARSON

Prentice
Hall

Glenview, Illinois
Needham, Massachusetts
Upper Saddle River, New Jersey

Connected Mathematics™ was developed at Michigan State University with the support of National Science Foundation Grant No. MDR 9150217.

This project was supported, in part,
by the
National Science Foundation
Opinions expressed are those of the authors
and not necessarily those of the Foundation

The Michigan State University authors and administration have agreed that all MSU royalties arising from this publication will be devoted to purposes supported by the Department of Mathematics and the MSU Mathematics Education Enrichment Fund.

Photo Acknowledgements: 5 © Kathy McLaughlin/The Image Works; 16 © David Shopper/Stock, Boston; 20 © Phyllis Graber Jensen/Stock, Boston; 21 Courtesy of the Pontiac Stadium Building Authority; 37 © Gary Benson/Tony Stone Images; 43 © Steve Kaufman/Peter Arnold, Inc.; 47 © Jean-Claude Lejeune/Stock, Boston; 53 (igloo) © Dave Rosenberg/Tony Stone Images; 53 (adobe) © Superstock, Inc.; 55 © Topham/The Image Works; 71 © Lionel Delevingne/Stock, Boston

ISBN 0-13-180821-4
1 2 3 4 5 6 7 8 9 10   07 06 05 04 03

The Connected Mathematics Project Staff

Project Directors

James T. Fey
University of Maryland

William M. Fitzgerald
Michigan State University

Susan N. Friel
University of North Carolina at Chapel Hill

Glenda Lappan
Michigan State University

Elizabeth Difanis Phillips
Michigan State University

Project Manager

Kathy Burgis
Michigan State University

Technical Coordinator

Judith Martus Miller
Michigan State University

Curriculum Development Consultants

David Ben-Chaim
Weizmann Institute

Alex Friedlander
Weizmann Institute

Eleanor Geiger
University of Maryland

Jane Mitchell
University of North Carolina at Chapel Hill

Anthony D. Rickard
Alma College

Collaborating Teachers/Writers

Mary K. Bouck
Portland, Michigan

Jacqueline Stewart
Okemos, Michigan

Graduate Assistants

Scott J. Baldridge
Michigan State University

Angie S. Eshelman
Michigan State University

M. Faaiz Gierdien
Michigan State University

Jane M. Keiser
Indiana University

Angela S. Krebs
Michigan State University

James M. Larson
Michigan State University

Ronald Preston
Indiana University

Tat Ming Sze
Michigan State University

Sarah Theule-Lubienski
Michigan State University

Jeffrey J. Wanko
Michigan State University

Evaluation Team

Mark Hoover
Michigan State University

Diane V. Lambdin
Indiana University

Sandra K. Wilcox
Michigan State University

Judith S. Zawojewski
National-Louis University

Teacher/Assessment Team

Kathy Booth
Waverly, Michigan

Anita Clark
Marshall, Michigan

Julie Faulkner
Traverse City, Michigan

Theodore Gardella
Bloomfield Hills, Michigan

Yvonne Grant
Portland, Michigan

Linda R. Lobue
Vista, California

Suzanne McGrath
Chula Vista, California

Nancy McIntyre
Troy, Michigan

Mary Beth Schmitt
Traverse City, Michigan

Linda Walker
Tallahassee, Florida

Software Developer

Richard Burgis
East Lansing, Michigan

Development Center Directors

Nicholas Branca
San Diego State University

Dianne Briars
Pittsburgh Public Schools

Frances R. Curcio
New York University

Perry Lanier
Michigan State University

J. Michael Shaughnessy
Portland State University

Charles Vonder Embse
Central Michigan University

Special thanks to the students and teachers at these pilot schools!

Baker Demonstration School
Evanston, Illinois

Bertha Vos Elementary School
Traverse City, Michigan

Blair Elementary School
Traverse City, Michigan

Bloomfield Hills Middle School
Bloomfield Hills, Michigan

Brownell Elementary School
Flint, Michigan

Catlin Gabel School
Portland, Oregon

Cherry Knoll Elementary School
Traverse City, Michigan

Cobb Middle School
Tallahassee, Florida

Courtade Elementary School
Traverse City, Michigan

Duke School for Children
Durham, North Carolina

DeVeaux Junior High School
Toledo, Ohio

East Junior High School
Traverse City, Michigan

Eastern Elementary School
Traverse City, Michigan

Eastlake Elementary School
Chula Vista, California

Eastwood Elementary School
Sturgis, Michigan

Elizabeth City Middle School
Elizabeth City, North Carolina

Franklinton Elementary School
Franklinton, North Carolina

Frick International Studies Academy
Pittsburgh, Pennsylvania

Gundry Elementary School
Flint, Michigan

Hawkins Elementary School
Toledo, Ohio

Hilltop Middle School
Chula Vista, California

Holmes Middle School
Flint, Michigan

Interlochen Elementary School
Traverse City, Michigan

Los Altos Elementary School
San Diego, California

Louis Armstrong Middle School
East Elmhurst, New York

McTigue Junior High School
Toledo, Ohio

National City Middle School
National City, California

Norris Elementary School
Traverse City, Michigan

Northeast Middle School
Minneapolis, Minnesota

Oak Park Elementary School
Traverse City, Michigan

Old Mission Elementary School
Traverse City, Michigan

Old Orchard Elementary School
Toledo, Ohio

Portland Middle School
Portland, Michigan

Reizenstein Middle School
Pittsburgh, Pennsylvania

Sabin Elementary School
Traverse City, Michigan

Shepherd Middle School
Shepherd, Michigan

Sturgis Middle School
Sturgis, Michigan

Terrell Lane Middle School
Louisburg, North Carolina

Tierra del Sol Middle School
Lakeside, California

Traverse Heights Elementary School
Traverse City, Michigan

University Preparatory Academy
Seattle, Washington

Washington Middle School
Vista, California

Waverly East Intermediate School
Lansing, Michigan

Waverly Middle School
Lansing, Michigan

West Junior High School
Traverse City, Michigan

Willow Hill Elementary School
Traverse City, Michigan

Contents

Filling and Wrapping

Baseballs, basketballs, and soccer balls are spheres, but they often come in boxes shaped like cubes. Why do you think these balls are packaged in this way?

Salt, juice concentrate, oatmeal, and tuna are often sold in packages shaped like cylinders. Why do you think these items are packaged in cylindrical containers instead of rectangular boxes?

At the Bijou theater, popcorn is sold in rectangular boxes with a height of 20 centimeters and a square base with 12-centimeter sides. At the Roxy theater, popcorn is sold in cylindrical boxes with a height of 20 centimeters and a diameter of 12 centimeters. Both theaters charge $2.50 for a box of popcorn. At which theater will you get the most popcorn for your money?

The way a product is packaged is important. Stores are filled with boxes, cans, bags, and bottles. An attractive or unique package can attract shoppers so they will take a closer look at the product.

Thinking about how products are packaged can make you a smarter consumer. For example, you can usually save money by purchasing products packaged in large quantities. You can help save natural resources by buying products that use a minimum amount of packaging material or that are packaged in boxes made from recycled material.

In this unit, you will look at two different measures involved in packaging. You will explore how much material it takes to *fill* a package and how much packaging material is needed to *wrap* a product. As you work through this unit, you will consider questions like those on the opposite page.

Mathematical Highlights

In *Filling and Wrapping* you will explore surface area and volume of objects, in particular, rectangular prisms, cylinders, cones, and spheres. The unit should help you to

- Understand volume as a measure of *filling* an object and surface area as a measure of *wrapping* an object;

- Develop strategies and formulas for finding the volume and surface area of objects including rectangular prisms and cylinders;

- Find patterns among the volumes of cylinders, cones, and spheres;

- Design flat patterns for rectangular prisms given certain specifications;

- Investigate the effects of varying the dimensions of rectangular prisms and cylinders on volume and surface area;

- Estimate the volume of irregular shapes by measuring the amount of water displaced by the solid; and

- Recognize and solve problems involving volume and surface area.

As you work on the problems of this unit, ask yourself questions about problem situations that involve volume and surface area: *What quantities are involved in the problem? Which measures of an object are involved—volume or surface area? Is an exact answer required? What method should I use to determine these measures? What strategies or formulas might help?*

Building Boxes

The most common type of package is the rectangular box. Rectangular boxes come filled with everything from cereal to shoes and from pizza to paper clips. Most rectangular boxes begin as flat sheets of cardboard. The sheets are cut and then folded into a box shape and glued or taped together.

1.1 Making Cubic Boxes

Some boxes are shaped like cubes. A **cube** is a three-dimensional shape with six identical square **faces**. What kinds of things might be packaged in cubic boxes?

In this problem, you will make **flat patterns** that can be folded to form boxes. The diagram on the left below shows one possible flat pattern for a cubic box.

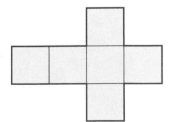
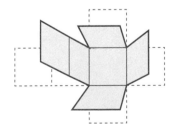

The boxes you will work with in this problem are shaped like unit cubes. A **unit cube** is a cube with **edges** that are 1 unit long. Cubes that are 1 inch on each edge are called inch cubes, and cubes that are 1 centimeter on each edge are called centimeter cubes.

A. How many different flat patterns can you make that will fold into a box shaped like a unit cube? Make a sketch of each pattern you find on inch grid paper. Test each pattern by cutting it out and folding it into a box.

B. Find the total area of each pattern.

■ Problem 1.1 Follow-Up

1. Choose one of your flat patterns from Problem 1.1, and make a copy of it on grid paper. Add the least possible number of flaps you need to be able to fold the pattern and glue it together to make a box with a lid that opens. The lid should have a flap that you tuck in to close the box. On your drawing indicate which flap will be part of the lid and which flaps will be glued. Cut your pattern out and fold it to make sure that it works.

2. Below is Benjamin's work for question 1. Does his pattern meet the requirements given in that question?

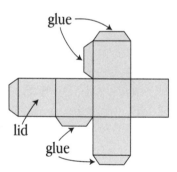

3. Copy Benjamin's flat pattern and add a different set of flaps so that his pattern meets the requirements in question 1.

Making Rectangular Boxes

Many boxes are not shaped like cubes. The box below has square ends, but the remaining faces are nonsquare rectangles. Next to the box is a flat pattern that could be folded to make the box.

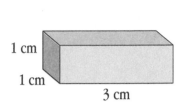
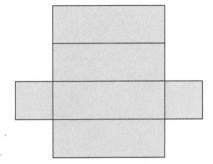

Problem 1.2

A. On grid paper, draw a flat pattern for a rectangular box that is *not* a cube. Each side length of your pattern should be a whole number of units. Then, make a different flat pattern for the same box. Test each pattern by cutting it out and folding it into a box.

B. Find the total area of each flat pattern you made in part A.

C. Describe the faces of the box formed from each flat pattern you made. What are the dimensions of each face?

D. How many unit cubes will fit into the box formed from each flat pattern you made? Explain how you got your answer.

■ Problem 1.2 Follow-Up

Choose one of your flat patterns from Problem 1.2, and make a copy of it on grid paper. Add the least possible number of flaps you need to be able to fold the pattern and glue it together to make a box with a lid that opens. The lid should have a flap that you tuck in to close the box. On your drawing indicate which flap will be part of the lid and which flaps will be glued.

1.3 Flattening a Box

A **rectangular prism** is a three-dimensional shape with six rectangular faces. A cube is a special type of rectangular prism. All the boxes you have made so far have been shaped like rectangular prisms. The size of a rectangular prism can be described by giving its dimensions—the length, the width, and the height.

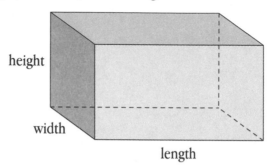

The **base** of a rectangular prism is the face on the bottom, or the face that rests on the table or floor. The length and width of a prism are the length and width of its rectangular base, and the height is the distance from the base of the prism to its top.

Amy is a packaging engineer at the Save-a-Tree packaging company. Mr. Shu asked Amy to come to his class and explain her job to his students. To help the class understand her work, she gave the students boxes and scissors and asked them to do some exploring.

> ### Problem 1.3
>
> Your teacher will give you a box.
>
> **A.** Find the dimensions of your box in centimeters.
>
> **B.** Use the dimensions you found in part A to make a flat pattern for your box on grid paper.
>
> **C.** Cut your box along the edges so that, when you lay it out flat, it will match your flat pattern from part B.

■ Problem 1.3 Follow-Up

1. Amy explained that one thing she considers when designing a box is the cost of the material. If the material for your box costs $\frac{1}{10}$ of a cent per square centimeter, what is the total cost of the material for your box? Why might this information be useful?

2. What other information or constraints do you think would be important to consider when designing a box?

Testing Flat Patterns

The flat patterns below were drawn by one of the engineers at the Save-a-Tree packaging company. The engineer lost his notes that indicated the dimensions of the boxes. Can you help him determine the dimensions?

Box P   **Box Q**   **Box R**

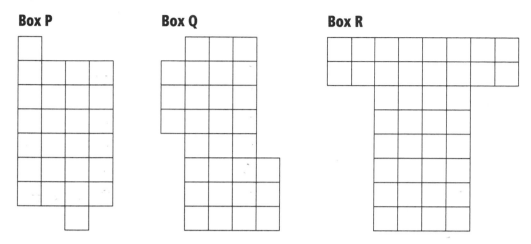

Problem 1.4

A. Cut out each pattern on Labsheet 1.4, and fold it to form a box.

B. Find the dimensions of each box.

C. How are the dimensions of each box related to the dimensions of its faces?

D. Find the total area of all the faces of each box.

E. Fill each box with unit cubes. How many cubes does it take to fill each box?

■ Problem 1.4 Follow-Up

Design a flat pattern for a box that has a different shape from box P (from Labsheet 1.4) but that holds the same number of cubes as box P.

As you work on these ACE questions, use your calculator whenever you need it.

Applications

1. An *open box* is a box without a top.

    a. On grid paper, sketch three different flat patterns for an open cubic box. Find the area of each flat pattern you found.

    b. On grid paper, sketch three different flat patterns for an open rectangular box (not a cubic box) with square ends. Find the area of each flat pattern you found.

In 2–5, tell whether the flat pattern could be folded along the lines to form a closed cubic box. If you are unsure, cut the pattern out of grid paper and experiment.

2.

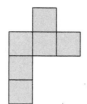

3.

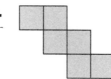

4.

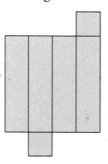

5.

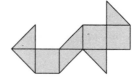

6. Which of these patterns could be folded along the lines to form a closed rectangular box?

    i.   ii.   iii.

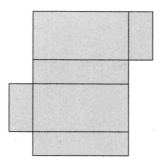
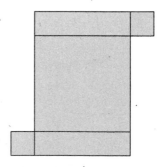

7. Do parts a–c for each pattern from question 6 that forms a box.

    a. Use the unit square shown to help you find the dimensions of the box.

                                             unit square

    b. Find the total area of all the faces of the box.

    c. Find the number of unit cubes it would take to fill the box.

8. This closed rectangular box does not have square ends.

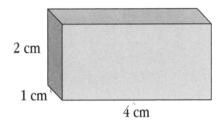

    a. What are the dimensions of the box?

    b. On grid paper, sketch two flat patterns for the box.

    c. Find the area of each flat pattern.

    d. Find the total area of all the faces of the box. How does your answer compare to the areas you found in part c?

Connections

9. a. What measurements do you need to find the area and perimeter of a rectangle? Explain how you would use these measurements to find the area and perimeter of a rectangle.

    b. What measurements do you need to find the area and perimeter of a square? Explain how you would use these measurements to find the area and perimeter of a square.

10. a. Draw a flat pattern for a rectangular box with dimensions 2 cm by 3 cm by 5 cm. Find the dimensions and area of each face.

b. What is the total area of all the faces of the box?

In 11–15, use the following information: A *hexomino* is a shape made of six identical squares connected along their sides. The flat patterns for a closed cubic box are examples of hexominos. Below are five different hexominos.

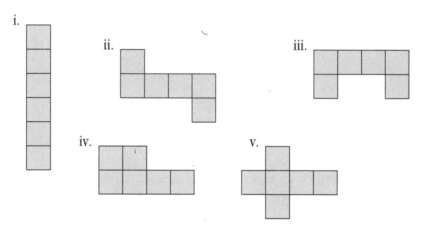

11. Find the perimeter of each hexomino shown above.

12. Which hexominos above could be folded to form a closed cubic box?

13. To which hexominos above can you add one square without changing the perimeter? For each hexomino that works, draw a diagram showing where the square could be added, and explain why the perimeter does not change.

14. To which hexominos above can you add two squares without changing the perimeter? For each hexomino that works, draw a diagram showing where the squares could be added, and explain why the perimeter does not change.

15. To which hexominos above can you add a square that changes the perimeter? For each hexomino that works, draw a diagram showing where the square could be added.

Extensions

16. A number cube is designed so that numbers on opposite sides add to 7. Write the integers from 1 to 6 on one of the flat patterns you found in Problem 1.1 so that it can be folded to form a number cube. You may want to test your pattern by cutting it out and folding it.

17. Could the flat pattern below be folded along the lines to form a rectangular box? If so, explain how.

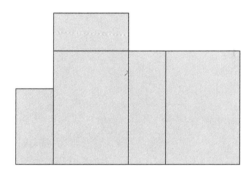

18. Could the flat pattern below be folded along the lines to form an open cubic box? If so, explain how.

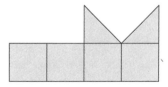

19. Examine the flat patterns you made for cubic boxes in Problem 1.1. Suppose you wanted to make boxes by tracing several copies of the same pattern onto a large sheet of cardboard and cutting them out. Which pattern would allow you to make the greatest number of boxes from a sheet of cardboard? Test your ideas by tiling a piece of grid paper with your box pattern. (*Tiling* is covering a flat surface with copies of a figure with no overlaps or gaps.)

Mathematical Reflections

In this investigation, you explored rectangular boxes, and you made flat patterns for boxes. You found the dimensions of a box, the total area of all its faces, and the number of unit cubes required to fill it. These questions will help you summarize what you have learned:

1 Suppose you were a packaging engineer. Explain why you might want to know the total area of all the faces of a rectangular box.

2 Explain how you would find the total area of all the faces of a rectangular box.

3 Explain how you would find the number of cubes it would take to fill a rectangular box.

4 What features must be the same for any flat pattern for a given box? What features might be different?

Think about your answers to these questions, discuss your ideas with other students and your teacher, and then write a summary of your findings in your journal.

Designing Packages

Finding the right box for a particular product requires a lot of thought and planning. A company must consider how much a box can hold and the amount and cost of the material needed to make the box.

The amount that a box can hold depends on its volume. The **volume** of a box is the number of unit cubes that would fill the box. The amount of material needed to make or cover a box depends on the box's surface area. The **surface area** of a box is the total area of all of its faces.

The box shown below has dimensions 1 centimeter by 3 centimeters by 1 centimeter. It would take three 1-centimeter cubes to fill this box, so the box has a volume of 3 cubic centimeters. Since it takes fourteen 1-centimeter grid squares to make the box, the box has a surface area of 14 square centimeters.

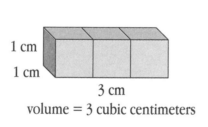

1 cm
1 cm
3 cm
volume = 3 cubic centimeters

surface area = 14 square centimeters

In this investigation, you will explore the possible surface areas for a rectangular box that holds a given amount. In other words, you will investigate the range of possible surface areas for boxes with a fixed volume.

2.1 Packaging Blocks

ABC Toy Company is planning to market a set of children's alphabet blocks. Each block is a cube with 1-inch edges, so each block has a volume of 1 cubic inch.

Problem 2.1

The company wants to arrange 24 blocks in the shape of a rectangular prism and then package them in a box that exactly fits the prism.

A. Find all the ways 24 cubes can be arranged into a rectangular prism. Make a sketch of each arrangement you find, and give its dimensions and surface area. It may help to organize your findings into a table like the one below.

Possible Arrangements of 24 Cubes

Length	Width	Height	Volume	Surface area	Sketch
			24 cubic inches		
			24 cubic inches		
			24 cubic inches		

B. Which of your arrangements requires the least material to make the box? Which requires the most material?

■ Problem 2.1 Follow-Up

Which arrangement would you recommend to ABC Toy Company? Write a short report giving your recommendation and explaining the reasons for your choice.

2.2 Saving Trees

Were you surprised to discover that 24 blocks can be packaged in ways that use quite different amounts of packaging material? By reducing the amount of material it uses, a company can save money, reduce waste, and conserve natural resources.

Both boxes have the same volume.

Problem 2.2

When packaging a given number of cubes, which rectangular arrangement uses the least amount of packaging material?

To help you answer this question, you can investigate some special cases and look for a pattern in the results. Explore the possible arrangements of the following numbers of cubes. For each number of cubes, try to find the arrangement that would require the least amount of packaging material.

| 8 cubes | 27 cubes | 12 cubes |

Use your findings to make a conjecture about the rectangular arrangement of cubes that requires the least packaging material.

■ Problem 2.2 Follow-Up

1. Test your conjecture from Problem 2.2 on some other examples, such as 30 cubes or 64 cubes. Does your conjecture work for the examples you tried? If not, change your conjecture so it works for any number of cubes. When you have a conjecture that you think is correct, give reasons why you think your conjecture is valid.

2. What rectangular arrangement of cubes uses the most packaging material? Why do you think this is so?

3. What is the surface area of the box below? Explain how you found your answer.

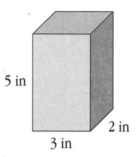

5 in
2 in
3 in

4. Suppose the box in question 3 were resting on a different face. How would this affect its surface area?

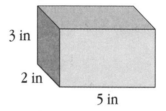

3 in
2 in
5 in

Did you know?

Area is expressed in *square units,* such as square inches or square centimeters. You can abbreviate square units by writing the abbreviation for the unit followed by a raised, or *superscripted,* 2. For example, an abbreviation for square inches is in^2, and an abbreviation for square centimeters is cm^2.

Volume is expressed in *cubic units,* such as cubic inches or cubic centimeters. You can abbreviate cubic units by writing the abbreviation for the unit followed by a superscripted 3. For example, an abbreviation for cubic inches is in^3, and an abbreviation for cubic centimeters is cm^3.

As you work on these ACE questions, use your calculator whenever you need it.

Applications

In 1–3, a rectangular prism made from inch cubes is pictured. Answer parts a–c.

1.   **2.**   **3.**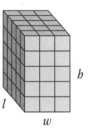

    a. What are the length, width, and height of the prism?

    b. How much material would be needed to make a box for the prism?

    c. How many blocks are in the prism?

4. Suppose you want to make a box to hold exactly thirty 1-inch cubes.

    a. Describe all the possible boxes you could make.

    b. Which box has the least surface area? Which has the greatest surface area?

    c. Why might you want to know the dimensions of the box with the least surface area?

5. a. Sketch a rectangular box with dimensions 2 cm by 3 cm by 6 cm.

    b. What is the surface area of your box?

    c. Sketch a flat pattern for your box. What is the relationship between the area of the flat pattern and the surface area of the box?

Connections

6. There is only one way to arrange five identical cubes into the shape of a rectangular prism.

    a. Sketch the rectangular prism made from five identical cubes.

    b. Give some other numbers of cubes that can be arranged into a rectangular prism in only one way. What kind of numbers are these?

7. **a.** Sketch every rectangular prism that can be made from ten identical cubes.

    b. Find the surface area of each prism you sketched in part a.

    c. Give the dimensions of the prism from part a that has the least surface area.

    d. Find one other number of blocks that has this same number of rectangular arrangements.

8. The dimensions of the recreation center floor are 150 ft by 45 ft, and the walls are 10 ft high. A gallon of paint will cover 400 ft^2. About how much paint is needed to paint the walls of the recreation center?

9. **a.** If a small can of paint will cover 1400 in^2, about how many cans are needed to paint the walls of the recreation center described in question 8?

    b. What factors might affect how much paint is actually used?

10. **a.** Graph the relationship between the area of the base and the height for your rectangular arrangements in Problem 2.1.

    b. Describe the relationship between the height and the area of the base.

    c. How might your graph be useful to the packaging engineer at ABC Toys?

11. The 1994 World Cup soccer championships were held in the United States. Some of the games were played in the Silverdome in Pontiac, Michigan. The dimensions of the soccer field in the Silverdome were 71 m by 115 m.

   a. How many square meters of turf were needed to cover the field?

   b. What were the dimensions of the field in feet? (1 in = 2.54 cm and 1 m = 100 cm)

Did you know?

The Pontiac Silverdome, like most domed stadiums, normally has a field made from artificial turf. However, the World Cup Soccer Host Committee required that the Silverdome be fitted with a natural grass field that could survive three weeks of soccer matches. The Detroit World Cup Bid Committee asked scientists at Michigan State University to help.

Because of the lack of natural light in the Silverdome, scientists had to design a turf system that could be grown outside the Silverdome and then brought inside and prepared for play. They grew the turf in about 2000 hexagonal pieces, each 7.5 feet wide. About two weeks before the first soccer game was to be played on the turf, the hexagonal pieces were brought inside and pieced together. Why do you think researchers chose hexagons rather than squares, rectangles, or some other shape?

Extensions

12. Many brands of soft drink are packaged in rectangular boxes of 24 cans.

    a. During the spring of 1993, a major cola company announced that they were going to package 24 cans into a more cube-like shape. Why might the company have done this?

    b. List all the ways 24 cans of soda could be arranged and packaged in a rectangular box. Which arrangement would you recommend that a soft drink company use? Why?

13. Slam Dunk Sporting Goods packages its basketballs in cubic boxes with 1-ft edges.

    a. Slam Dunk ships basketballs from its factory to stores all over the country. To ship the balls, the company packs 12 basketballs (in their boxes) into a large rectangular shipping box. Find the dimensions of every possible shipping box into which the boxes of balls would exactly fit.

    b. Find the surface area of each shipping box you found in part a.

    c. Slam Dunk uses the shipping box that requires the least material. Which shipping box do they use?

    d. Slam Dunk decides to ship basketballs in boxes of 24. They want to use the shipping box that requires the least material. Find the dimensions of the box they should use. How much more packaging material is needed to ship 24 balls than to ship 12 balls?

Mathematical Reflections

In this investigation, you arranged cubes in the shape of rectangular prisms, and you found the arrangements with the least and greatest surface area. These questions will help you summarize what you have learned:

1 For a given number of cubes, what arrangement will give a rectangular prism with the least surface area? What arrangement will give a rectangular prism with the greatest surface area? Use specific examples to illustrate your ideas.

2 Describe how you can find the surface area of a rectangular prism.

Think about your answers to these questions, discuss your ideas with other students and your teacher, and then write a summary of your findings in your journal.

INVESTIGATION 3

Finding Volumes of Boxes

In the last investigation, you started with a fixed number of cubes and explored the various ways you could arrange them to form a rectangular prism. In this investigation, you will start with boxes shaped like rectangular prisms and determine how many unit cubes they will hold.

3.1 Filling Rectangular Boxes

To package its products, a company may have boxes custom-made. However, a company can save money if it buys ready-made boxes. The Save-a-Tree packaging company sells ready-made boxes in several sizes.

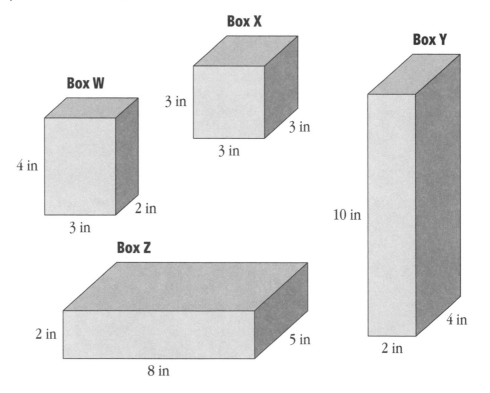

Box W — 4 in, 2 in, 3 in

Box X — 3 in, 3 in, 3 in

Box Y — 10 in, 2 in, 4 in

Box Z — 2 in, 5 in, 8 in

Problem 3.1

ABC Toy Company is considering using one of Save-a-Tree's ready-made boxes to ship their blocks. Each block is a 1-inch cube. ABC needs to know how many blocks will fit into each box and the surface area of each box.

A. How many blocks will fit in each of Save-a-Tree's ready-made boxes? Explain how you got your answer.

B. What is the surface area of each box? Explain how you got your answer.

■ Problem 3.1 Follow-Up

1. How many cubes would fit in a single layer at the bottom of each box in Problem 3.1?

2. How many *identical layers* of cubes could be stacked in each box?

3. The number of unit cubes that fit in a box is the volume of the box. For each box in Problem 3.1, consider the box's dimensions, the number of cubes in a layer, the number of layers, and the volume. What connections do you see among these measurements?

4. Suppose box Y were laid on its side so its base was 4 inches by 10 inches and its height was 2 inches. Would this affect the volume of the box? Explain your reasoning.

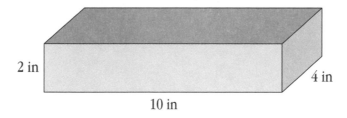

2 in   4 in

10 in

3.2 Burying Garbage

The city of Greendale has set aside a piece of land on which to bury its garbage. The city plans to dig a rectangular hole with a base measuring 500 feet by 200 feet and a depth of 75 feet.

The population of Greendale is 100,000. It has been estimated that, on average, a family of four throws away 0.4 cubic foot of compacted garbage a day. How could this information help Greendale evaluate the plan for a waste site?

Problem 3.2

A. How much garbage will this site hold?

B. How long will it take before the hole is filled?

■ Problem 3.2 Follow-Up

What suggestions would you make to the Greendale city council about their plan?

3.3 Filling Fancy Boxes

Prisms come in many different shapes. A **prism** is a three-dimensional shape with a top and bottom that are congruent polygons, and faces that are parallelograms. The boxes you have investigated so far in this unit have been shaped like rectangular prisms. A prism is named for the shape of its base. For example, the base of a rectangular prism is a rectangle, and the base of a triangular prism is a triangle. Some prisms are shown below.

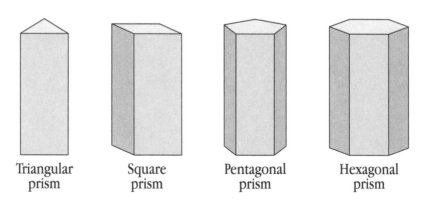

Triangular   Square   Pentagonal   Hexagonal
prism   prism   prism   prism

You have seen that you can find the volume of a rectangular prism by thinking about the number of unit cubes that would fit inside the prism. In this problem, you will see if a similar method will work for finding the volume of a nonrectangular prism. First, you need to make some paper prisms. (These paper prisms are actually prism-shaped boxes that are open at the top and bottom.)

Making paper prisms
- Start with four identical sheets of paper.
- Fold one of the sheets of paper into three congruent rectangles. Tape the paper into the shape of a triangular prism.

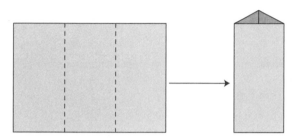

- Fold a second sheet of paper into four congruent rectangles, and tape it into the shape of a square prism.
- Fold and tape the remaining two sheets of paper as shown below to form pentagonal and hexagonal prisms.

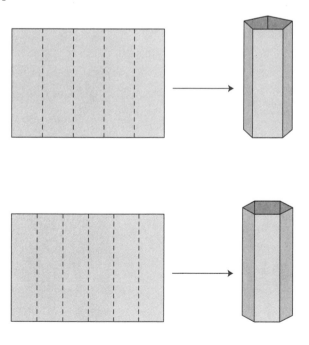

Problem 3.3

In Problems 3.1 and 3.2, you saw that you could find the volume of a rectangular prism by figuring out how many cubes would fit in a single layer at the bottom of the prism and then figuring out how many layers it would take to fill the prism. Do you think this layering method would work for finding volumes of different types of prisms?

A. Find the volumes of the triangular, square, pentagonal, and hexagonal prisms you made in cubic centimeters. Describe the method you use.

B. Imagine that each of your paper prisms had a top and a bottom. How would you find the surface area of each prism? Which of the four prisms would have the greatest surface area?

■ **Problem 3.3 Follow-Up**

1. Do parts a and b for each paper prism you made.
   a. Set the paper prism on its base on a sheet of centimeter grid paper. Trace the prism's base. Look at the centimeter squares inside your tracing. How many cubes would fit in one layer at the bottom of the prism? Consider whole cubes and parts of cubes.
   b. How many layers of centimeter cubes would it take to completely fill the prism?
2. What connections can you make between the area of a prism's base, the height of the prism, and the volume of the prism?
3. Suppose you used the same size sheets of paper to make prisms with 7 sides, 8 sides, 9 sides, and so on. What would happen to the shape of the prism as the number of sides increased? What would happen to the volume of the prism as the number of sides increased?

Save your paper prisms for the next investigation.

As you work on these ACE questions, use your calculator whenever you need it.

Applications

In 1–3, a rectangular prism made from inch cubes is pictured. Answer parts a–c.

1.

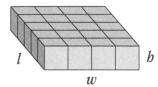

2.

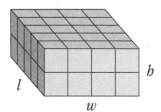

3.

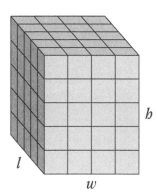

    a.   What are the length, width, and height of the prism?

    b.   What is the volume of the prism? Describe how you found the volume.

    c.   What is the surface area of the prism? Describe how you found the surface area.

4. a. How many cubes are needed to fill the closed box below?

b. What is the surface area of the box?

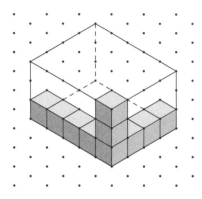

In 5–7, find the volume and surface area of the closed box.

5.

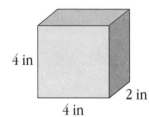

4 in

4 in

2 in

6.

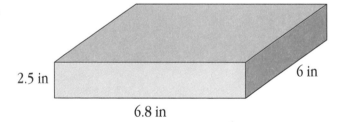

2.5 in

6.8 in

6 in

7.

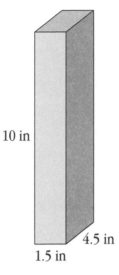

10 in

4.5 in

1.5 in

8. a. Make a sketch of a closed box with dimensions 2 cm by 3 cm by 5 cm.

b. How many centimeter cubes would fit in one layer at the bottom of the box?

c. How many layers would be needed to fill the box?

d. Find the volume of the box.

e. Find the surface area of the box.

9. Mr. Singh's classroom is 20 ft wide, 30 ft long, and 10 ft high.

a. Sketch a scale model of Mr. Singh's classroom. Label the dimensions of the classroom on your sketch.

b. Find the volume of Mr. Singh's classroom. Why might this information be useful to know?

c. Find the total area of the walls, the floor, and the ceiling. Why might this information be useful to know?

10. **a.** Sketch a prism with a base of area 40 cm^2 and a height of 5 cm.

b. What is the volume of the prism you drew?

c. Do you think everyone in your class drew the same prism? Explain.

d. Do you think the prisms your classmates drew have the same volume as your prism? Explain.

11. Below are side and top views of a triangular prism with ends that are equilateral triangles.

a. Describe two ways you could find the volume of the prism. What is the volume?

b. Describe two ways you could find the surface area of the prism. What is the surface area?

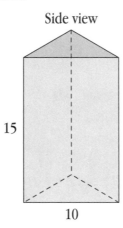

Side view

15

10

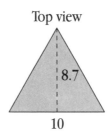

Top view

8.7

10

Connections

12. In Problem 3.1, boxes Y and Z have the same volume. Describe the dimensions of another rectangular prism with this same volume but a smaller surface area.

13. a. On isometric dot paper, sketch a closed box with dimensions 4 by 1 by 3.

b. How many unit cubes would fit in a single layer at the bottom of the box you drew?

c. How many layers of unit cubes would be needed to fill the box?

d. Find the volume of the box.

e. Find the surface area of the box.

f. Is there a box with the same volume but less surface area? Explain your answer.

g. Is there a box with the same volume but greater surface area? Explain your answer.

14. The city of Rubberville plans to dig a rectangular landfill. The landfill will have a base with dimensions 700 ft by 200 ft and a depth of 85 ft.

a. How many cubic feet of garbage will the landfill hold?

b. What information would you need to determine how long the landfill can be used until it is full?

c. An excavator was hired to dig the hole for the landfill. How many cubic yards of dirt will he have to haul away?

15. a. Look for an object in your classroom or neighborhood with a volume of about 60 ft^3. Explain how you estimated the volume of the object.

b. Look for an object in your classroom or neighborhood with a volume of about 60 cm^3. Explain how you estimated the volume of the object.

16. Find four rectangular boxes in your home.

    a. Find the dimensions of each box.

    b. Find the volume and surface area of each box.

    c. Is it possible for two boxes to have the same volume but different surface areas? Explain why or why not.

    d. Why do you think most products are not packaged in the shape that uses the least packaging material?

    e. Choose one of the four boxes. See if you can design a box with the same volume as the box you chose but with a smaller surface area. That is, see if you can design a more efficient package.

17. **a.** Look for objects outside of your classroom that are shaped like prisms. Find three objects that are rectangular prisms and three objects that are nonrectangular prisms.

    b. Without measuring, estimate the volume of each object.

    c. How could you check the volumes you found in part b?

Extensions

18. The drawing below shows a prism with an odd-shaped top and bottom and rectangular sides. The top and bottom each have an area of 10 cm², and the height is 4 cm. What is the volume of the prism? Explain how you found the volume and why you think your method works.

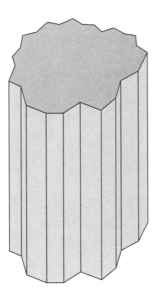

Mathematical Reflections

In this investigation, you developed methods for finding volumes of rectangular and nonrectangular prisms. These questions will help you summarize what you have learned:

1 What is the relationship between the number of unit cubes needed to fill a prism-shaped box and the volume of the box?

2 Describe how you can find the volume of any prism.

Think about your answers to these questions, discuss your ideas with other students and your teacher, and then write a summary of your findings in your journal.

Cylinders

So far in this unit, you have studied boxes shaped like prisms. There are many packages and containers that are not shaped like prisms. For example, salt, juice concentrate, oatmeal, and tuna are often sold in packages shaped like cylinders. A cylinder is a three-dimensional shape with a top and bottom that are congruent circles.

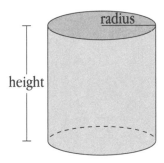

As with a prism, the bottom of a cylinder is called the *base,* and the distance from the base to the top is called the *height.* You can describe a cylinder by giving its dimensions. The *dimensions* of a cylinder are the radius of its base (or top) and its height.

Did you know?

Cylindrical cans often contain liquids. The volume, or *capacity,* of containers that hold liquids are often given in units like quarts, gallons, liters, and milliliters. Although volumes given in these units do not tell you how many unit cubes a container will hold, these units are based on cubic measures. For example, a gallon equals 231 cubic inches. In Investigation 7, you will figure out the cubic equivalent of 1 milliliter.

Filling a Cylinder

The *volume* of a container is the number of unit cubes it will hold. In the last investigation, you saw that you could find the volume of a prism-shaped box by figuring out how many unit cubes will fit in a single layer at the bottom of the box and then multiplying by the total number of layers needed to fill the box. In this problem, you will develop a method for determining how many cubes will fit inside a cylinder.

Problem 4.1

Make a cylinder by taping together the ends of a sheet of paper. Use the same size paper you used to make the prism shapes in Problem 3.3.

A. Set the cylinder on its base on a sheet of centimeter grid paper. Trace the cylinder's base. Look at the centimeter squares inside your tracing. How many cubes would fit in one layer at the bottom of the cylinder? Consider whole cubes and parts of cubes.

B. How many layers of cubes would it take to fill the cylinder?

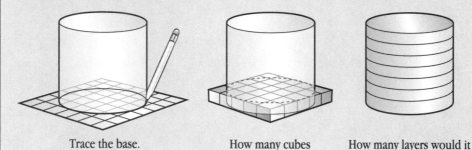

Trace the base.

How many cubes would fit in one layer?

How many layers would it take to fill the cylinder?

C. What is the volume of the cylinder?

■ **Problem 4.1 Follow-Up**

1. How can you use the dimensions of the cylinder to help you estimate its volume more accurately? Explain.

2. How does the volume of the cylinder compare to the volumes of the prisms you made in Problem 3.3?

4.2 Making a Cylinder from a Flat Pattern

In the last problem, you developed a strategy for finding the volume of a cylinder. In this problem, you will develop a strategy for finding the surface area of a cylinder. To do this problem, you will need Labsheet 4.2, which shows a flat pattern for a cylinder.

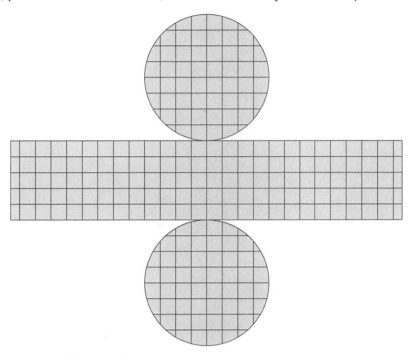

Problem 4.2

Cut out the flat pattern from Labsheet 4.2. Try to cut the pattern so there is a small connector between each circle and the rectangle.

A. What will the dimensions of the cylinder be?

B. What will the surface area of the cylinder be? Explain how you got your answer.

C. Tape the flat pattern together to form a cylinder. How many centimeter cubes will exactly fit in one layer at the bottom of the cylinder? How many cubes will exactly fill the cylinder?

■ Problem 4.2 Follow-Up

1. How are the dimensions of the circles and the rectangle in the flat pattern related to the dimensions of the cylinder?

2. How can you use the dimensions of a cylinder to calculate its volume?

3. How can you use the dimensions of a cylinder to calculate its surface area?

Designing a New Juice Container

Fruit Tree juice company packages its most popular drink, apple-prune juice, in small cylindrical cans. Each can is 8 centimeters high and has a radius of 2 centimeters.

Recent sales reports indicate that sales of Fruit Tree juice are falling, while sales of juice sold by a competitor, the Wrinkled Prune company, are on the rise. Market researchers at Fruit Tree determine that Wrinkled Prune's success is due to its new rectangular juice boxes. Fruit Tree decides to try packaging their juice in rectangular boxes.

Problem 4.3

Fruit Tree wants the new rectangular box to have the same volume as the current cylindrical can.

A. On centimeter grid paper, make a flat pattern for a box that would hold the same amount of juice as the cylindrical can.

B. Cut out your flat pattern. Use colored pencils or markers to design the outside of the box so it will appeal to potential customers. When you are finished, fold and tape your pattern to form a box.

C. Give the dimensions of your box. Are there other possibilities for the dimensions? Explain.

■ **Problem 4.3 Follow-Up**

1. Compare your juice box with the boxes made by your classmates. Which rectangular box shape do you think would make the best juice container? Why?

2. Make a flat pattern for the current cylindrical can.

3. Compare the surface area of the cylindrical can to the surface area of your juice box. Which container has greater surface area?

As you work on these ACE questions, use your calculator whenever you need it.

Applications

1. A cylindrical storage tank has a radius of 15 ft and a height of 30 ft.

   a. Make a sketch of the tank and label its dimensions.

   b. What is the volume of the tank?

   c. What is the surface area of the tank?

2. A cylinder has a radius of 3 cm. Sand is poured into the cylinder to form a layer 1 cm deep.

   a. What is the volume of sand in the cylinder?

   b. If the height of the cylinder is 20 cm, how many layers of sand—each 1 cm deep—are needed to fill the cylinder?

   c. What is the volume of the cylinder?

3. A soft drink can is a cylinder with a radius of 3 cm and a height of 12 cm. Ms. Doyle's classroom is 6 m wide, 8 m long, and 3 m high. Estimate the number of soft drink cans that would fit inside Ms. Doyle's classroom. Explain how you found your estimate.

4. Below is a scale model of a flat pattern for a cylinder.

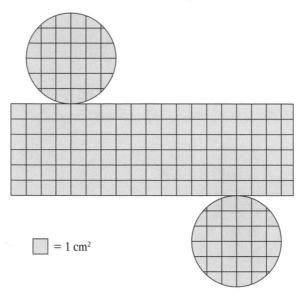

☐ = 1 cm²

    a. When the pattern is assembled, what will the volume of the cylinder be?

    b. What will the surface area of the cylinder be?

5. You are the manager of a new movie theater. You need to order popcorn boxes, and you must decide between a cylindrical box and a rectangular box. The cylindrical box has a height of 20 cm and a radius of 7 cm, and the rectangular box has a height of 20 cm and a square base with 12-cm sides. The price of each box is based on the amount of material needed to make the box. The theater plans to charge $2.75 for popcorn, regardless of the shape of the box.

    a. Find the volume and surface area of each container.

    b. Which box would you choose? Give the reasons for your choice. What additional information might help you make a better decision?

Connections

6. How is finding the area of a circle related to finding the volume of a cylinder?

7. Find three different cylindrical objects in your home. For each cylinder, record the dimensions and calculate the volume.

8. A pipeline for carrying oil is 5000 km long and has an inside diameter of 20 cm.

a. How many cubic centimeters of oil would it take to fill 1 km of the pipeline? (1 km = 100,000 cm)

b. How many cubic centimeters of oil would it take to fill the entire pipeline?

9. Carlos wants to build a rectangular hot tub that is 4 ft high and holds 1000 ft^3 of water. What could the dimensions of the base of Carlos's hot tub be?

10. The Buy-and-Go Mart sells soft drinks in three sizes. Which size is the best buy? Explain your answer.

12 oz	18 oz	32 oz
$1.25	$1.75	$3.00

11. Tell what features of a cylinder could be measured in the given units.

a. cm   **b.** cm^2 **c.** cm^3

Extensions

12. A cylindrical can is packed securely in a box as shown at right. The height of the box is 10 cm, and the sides of its square base measure 2 cm.

    a. Find the radius and height of the can.

    b. What is the volume of the empty space between the can and the box?

    c. Find the ratio of the volume of the can to the volume of the box.

    d. Make up a similar example with a different size can and box. What is the ratio of the volume of the can to the volume of the box for your example? How does the ratio compare to the ratio you got in part c?

13. Start with two identical sheets of paper. Tape the long sides of one sheet together to form a cylinder. Form a cylinder from the second sheet by taping the short sides together. Imagine that each cylinder has a top and a bottom.

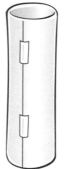

    a. Which cylinder has greater volume? Explain your reasoning.

    b. Which cylinder has greater surface area? Explain your reasoning.

Mathematical Reflections

In this investigation, you developed methods for finding the volume and surface area of a cylinder. These questions will help you summarize what you have learned:

1. Describe how you can find the volume of a cylinder.

2. Describe how you can find the surface area of a cylinder.

3. Discuss the similarities and differences in the methods for finding the volume of a cylinder, a rectangular prism, and a nonrectangular prism.

4. Discuss the similarities and differences in the methods for finding the surface area of a cylinder, a rectangular prism, and a nonrectangular prism.

Think about your answers to these questions, discuss your ideas with other students and your teacher, and then write a summary of your findings in your journal.

Cones and Spheres

Many common and important three-dimensional objects are not shaped like prisms or cylinders. For example, ice cream is often served in *cones.* The planet we live on is very nearly a *sphere.*

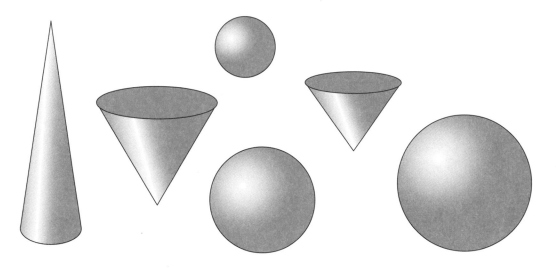

Cones come in many shapes and sizes—from tall and thin to short and wide. As with a cylinder and a prism, we can describe a cone by giving its dimensions. The *dimensions* of a cone are the radius of its circular end and its height.

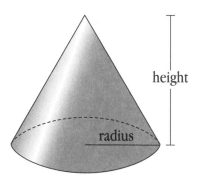

Although spheres may differ in size, they are all the same shape. We can describe a sphere by giving its radius.

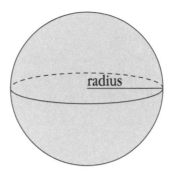

In this investigation, you will explore ways to determine the volume of cones and spheres.

5.1 Comparing Spheres and Cylinders

In this problem, you will make a sphere and a cylinder with the same radius and height and then compare their volumes. (The "height" of a sphere is just its diameter.) You can use the relationship you observe to help you develop a method for finding the volume of a sphere.

Did you know?

The Earth is nearly a sphere. You may have heard that, until Christopher Columbus's voyage in 1492, most people believed the Earth was flat. Actually, as early as the fourth century B.C., scientists in Greece and Egypt had figured out that the Earth was round. They observed the shadow of the Earth as it passed across the Moon during a lunar eclipse. It was clear that the shadow was round. Combining this observation with evidence gathered from observing constellations, these scientists concluded that the Earth was indeed spherical. In fact, in the third century B.C., Eratosthenes, a scientist from Alexandria, Egypt, was actually able to estimate the circumference of the Earth.

- Using modeling dough, make a sphere with a diameter between 2 inches and 3.5 inches.

- Using a strip of transparent plastic, make a cylinder with an open top and bottom that fits snugly around your sphere. Trim the height of the cylinder to match the height of the sphere. Tape the cylinder together so that it remains rigid.

- Now, flatten the sphere so that it fits snugly in the bottom of the cylinder. Mark the height of the flattened sphere on the cylinder.

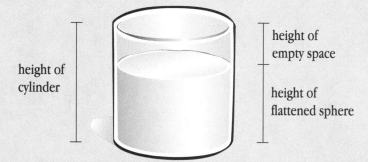

A. Measure and record the height of the cylinder, the height of the empty space, and the height of the flattened sphere.

B. What is the relationship between the volume of the sphere and the volume of the cylinder?

Remove the modeling dough from the cylinder, and save the cylinder for the next problem.

▣ Problem 5.1 Follow-Up

Compare your results with the results of a group that made a larger or smaller sphere. Did the other group find the same relationship between the volume of the sphere and the volume of the cylinder?

Comparing Cones and Cylinders

In the last problem, you discovered the relationship between the volume of a sphere and the volume of a cylinder. In this problem, you will look for a relationship between the volume of a cone and the volume of a cylinder.

Problem 5.2

- Roll a piece of stiff paper into a cone shape so that the tip touches the bottom of your cylinder.

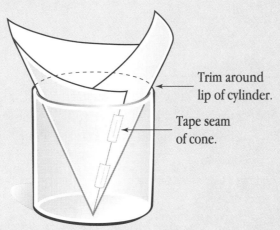

Trim around lip of cylinder.

Tape seam of cone.

- Tape the cone shape along the seam and trim it to form a cone with the same height as the cylinder.

- Fill the cone to the top with sand or rice, and empty the contents into the cylinder. Repeat this as many times as needed to completely fill the cylinder.

What is the relationship between the volume of the cone and the volume of the cylinder?

■ **Problem 5.2 Follow-Up**

If a cone, a cylinder, and a sphere have the same radius and the same height, what is the relationship between the volumes of the three shapes?

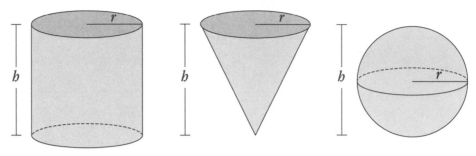

5.3 **Melting Ice Cream**

Olga and Serge buy ice cream from Chilly's Ice Cream Parlor. They think about buying an ice cream cone to bring back to Olga's little sister but decide the ice cream would melt before they got back home. Serge wonders, "If the ice cream all melts into the cone, will it fill the cone?"

> **Problem 5.3**
>
> Olga gets a scoop of ice cream in a cone, and Serge gets a scoop in a cylindrical cup. Each container has a height of 8 centimeters and a radius of 4 centimeters, and each scoop of ice cream is a sphere with a radius of 4 centimeters.
>
>
>
> **A.** If Serge allows his ice cream to melt, will it fill his cup exactly? Explain.
>
> **B.** If Olga allows her ice cream to melt, will it fill her cone exactly? Explain.

■ **Problem 5.3 Follow-Up**

How many scoops of ice cream of the size above can be packed into each container?

As you work on these ACE questions, use your calculator whenever you need it.

Applications

1. The city of La Agua has water storage tanks in three different shapes: a cylinder, a cone, and a sphere. Each tank has a radius of 20 ft and a height of 40 ft.

    a. Sketch each tank, and label its dimensions.

    b. What is the volume of the cylindrical tank?

    c. What is the volume of the conical tank?

    d. What is the volume of the spherical tank?

2. a. Find the volume of the cylinder, cone, and sphere shown below.

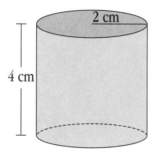
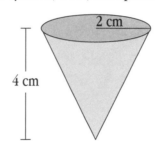
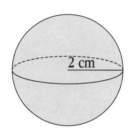

    b. How do the volumes of the three shapes compare?

3. An ice cream cone has a radius of 1 in and a height of 5 in. If a scoop of ice cream is a sphere with a radius of 1 in, how many scoops can be packed into the cone?

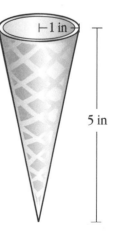

4. The track-and-field club is planning a frozen yogurt sale to raise money for new equipment. The club needs to buy containers to hold the yogurt. They must choose between the cup and cone shown below. The containers cost the same amount of money. The club plans to charge customers $1.25 for a serving of yogurt. Which container should the club buy? Why?

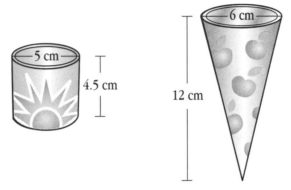

5. Fernando collected popcorn containers from several local movie theaters and recorded the prices and dimensions of the containers. Which is the best buy? Explain your answer.

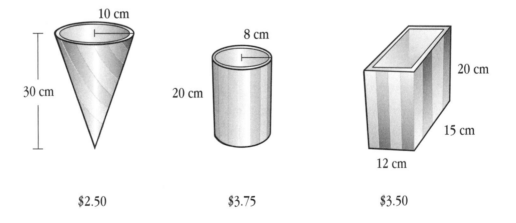

Connections

6. A soft drink can is a cylinder with a radius of 3 cm and a height of 12 cm.

    a. Sketch a soft drink can, and label its dimensions.

    b. What is the circumference of the can?

    c. What is the volume of the can?

    d. What is the surface area of the can?

    e. How many cans of soda would it take to fill a liter bottle? (A liter bottle contains 1000 cm^3.)

Extensions

7. Some Inuit Indians build igloos shaped like hemispheres (halves of a sphere). Some Hopi Indians in Arizona build adobes shaped like rectangular boxes. Suppose an igloo has an inner diameter of 40 ft.

    a. Describe the shape of a Hopi dwelling that would provide the same amount of living space as the igloo described above.

    b. For a Hopi dwelling to have the same amount of floor space as the igloo described above, what should the dimensions of the floor be?

8. Laurie made a scale model of a submarine for her science class.

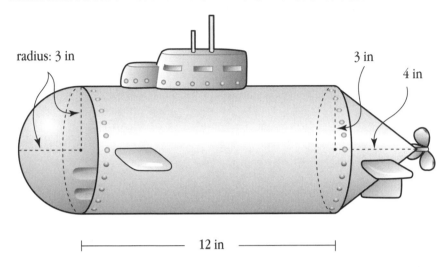

radius: 3 in

3 in

4 in

12 in

a. What is the volume of Laurie's model?

b. If 1 in on the model represents 100 ft on the actual submarine, what is the volume of the actual submarine?

9. a. Give the dimensions of the largest sphere that will fit inside a cubic box with 5-cm edges.

b. Give the dimensions of the largest cylinder that will fit inside a cubic box with 5-cm edges.

c. Give the dimensions of the largest cone that will fit inside a cubic box with 5-cm edges.

d. Which shape—sphere, cylinder, or cone—fits best inside the cubic box? That is, for which shape is there the least space between the shape and the box?

10. The edges of a cube measure 10 cm. Describe the dimensions of a cylinder and a cone with the same volume as the cube. (Hint: Starting with the cylinder is easier.) Explain your reasoning.

11. Pearl measures the circumference of a sphere and finds that it is 54 cm. What is the volume of the sphere? Explain.

12. The shapes below are pyramids. A pyramid is named for the shape of its base. The left shape is a triangular pyramid, the center shape is a square pyramid, and the right shape is a pentagonal pyramid. The sides of all pyramids are triangles.

a. As the number of sides in the base of a pyramid increases, what happens to the shape of the pyramid?

b. Describe a method for finding the surface area of a pyramid.

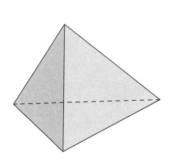 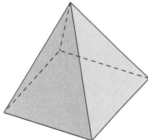 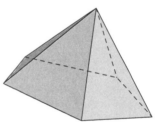

Mathematical Reflections

In this investigation, you studied the relationships between the volumes of a cone, a sphere, and a cylinder with the same radius and height. These questions will help you summarize what you have learned:

1. If a cone, a cylinder, and a sphere have the same radius and height, describe the relationships among the volume of the cone, the volume of the sphere, and the volume of the cylinder. Use examples and sketches to illustrate your answer.

2. If you know the radius of a sphere, how can you find the sphere's volume?

3. If you know the radius and height of a cone, how can you find the cone's volume?

Think about your answers to these questions, discuss your ideas with other students and your teacher, and then write a summary of your findings in your journal.

Scaling Boxes

Discarded paper, plastic, and glass is not the only urban-waste disposal problem. Decaying organic waste from food, grass, and leaves gives off unpleasant odors and explosive methane gas.

WE SHIP OURS FROM DECKVILLE TO LYLEPORT.

REALLY? WE SHIP OURS FROM LYLEPORT TO DECKVILLE.

TOXIC WASTES

HAZARDOUS MATERIALS

© 1991 by Sidney Harris. From *You Want Proof? I'll Give You Proof!* W. H. Freeman, New York.

Composting is a method for turning organic waste into rich soil. Composting has been used for thousands of years on farms and in gardens. Today, many people have indoor compost boxes that break down kitchen waste quickly and with little odor. The secret is in the worms!

Recipe for a 1-2-3 Compost Box

- Start with an open rectangular wood box that is 1 foot high, 2 feet wide, and 3 feet long. We call this a *1-2-3 box.*
- Mix 10 pounds of shredded newspaper with 15 quarts of water, and put the mixture in the 1-2-3 box.
- Add a few handfuls of soil.
- Add about 1000 redworms (about 1 pound).

Every day, mix collected kitchen waste with the soil in the box. The worms will do the rest of the work, turning the waste into new soil. A 1-2-3 box will decompose about 0.5 pound of garbage each day.

Source: Woldumar Nature Center, Lansing, Michigan.

Building a Bigger Box

Deshondra chose composting as the topic of her science project. She plans to build a compost box at home and to keep records of the amount of soil produced over several weeks.

Problem 6.1

Deshondra wants her compost box to be larger than the 1-2-3 box. She decides to double each edge of the 1-2-3 box.

A. Use grid paper to make scale models of a 1-2-3 box and Deshondra's 2-4-6 box. The boxes should have open tops.

B. Deshondra wants to increase the composting capacity of her box by the same factor as the volume. How much shredded paper and water will she need for her 2-4-6 compost box?

C. How many worms will she need?

D. How much plywood will she need to build the box?

E. How many pounds of garbage will the box be able to decompose in one day?

Save your model of the 1-2-3 box for the next problem.

■ Problem 6.1 Follow-Up

1. Find the ratio of the length of each side of the 1-2-3 box to the length of the corresponding side of the 2-4-6 box.

2. Find the ratio of the surface area of the 1-2-3 box to the surface area of the 2-4-6 box.

3. Find the ratio of the volume of the 1-2-3 box to the volume of the 2-4-6 box.

6.2 Scaling Up the Compost Box

Ms. Fernandez's class decides that building and maintaining a compost box would be a fascinating project. One student suggests that they could earn money for a class trip by selling the worms and soil they produce to a local nursery.

The class estimates that they throw away about 1 pound of organic waste each day, rather than the 0.5 pound specified in the 1-2-3 box recipe. They need to adjust the recipe to build a box large enough to decompose all the garbage they will produce.

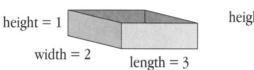

height = 1
width = 2
length = 3

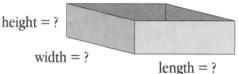

height = ?
width = ?
length = ?

Problem 6.2

How could Ms. Fernandez's class scale up the recipe for the 1-2-3 box to make a box that will decompose 1 pound of organic waste each day?

A. What box dimensions would give the required space for the new quantity of organic waste?

B. Use grid paper to make a scale model of a box that would decompose 1 pound of garbage per day. The box should have an open top.

■ Problem 6.2 Follow-Up

1. How much plywood will the class need to construct their box?

2. How much shredded paper and water will they need?

3. How many worms will they need?

Looking at Similar Prisms

In *Stretching and Shrinking,* you studied similar two-dimensional figures. The ideas you learned in that unit also apply to three-dimensional figures. For example, two rectangular prisms are similar if the ratios of the lengths of corresponding edges are equal.

The *scale factor* is the number that each dimension of one rectangular prism must be multiplied by to get the dimensions of a similar prism. For example, a 1-2-3 box is similar to a 2-4-6 box. The scale factor from the small box to the large box is 2, because the edge lengths of the small box must be multiplied by 2 to get the corresponding edge lengths of the large box.

Problem 6.3

A. Find three other rectangular boxes that are similar to a 1-2-3 box, and give their dimensions. Give the scale factor from a 1-2-3 box to each box you find.

B. 1. Calculate the surface area of each box you found in part A, and tell how the result compares to the surface area of a 1-2-3 box.

   2. How is the change in surface area from a 1-2-3 box to a similar box related to the scale factor from the 1-2-3 box to the similar box?

C. 1. Calculate the volume of each box you found in part A, and tell how the result compares to the volume of a 1-2-3 box.

   2. How is the change in volume from a 1-2-3 box to a similar box related to the scale factor from the 1-2-3 box to the similar box?

◼ Problem 6.3 Follow-Up

Are all rectangular prisms similar? Explain your answer.

As you work on these ACE questions, use your calculator whenever you need it. Remember that height is the first number when dimensions of a box are given.

Applications

1. a. What is the volume of a 1-2-2 box?

b. What is the surface area of a closed 1-2-2 box?

2. a. What is the volume of a 1.5-1.5-3 box?

b. What is the surface area of a closed 1.5-1.5-3 box?

3. a. What is the volume of a 2-4-1 box?

b. What is the surface area of a closed 2-4-1 box?

4. a. Make a sketch of an open 2-2-3 box and an open 2-2-6 box. Label the edges of the boxes.

b. Find the volume of each box in part a.

c. Find the surface area of each box in part a.

d. If you wanted to adapt the 1-2-3 compost box recipe for the boxes in part a, how many worms and how much paper and water would you need for each box?

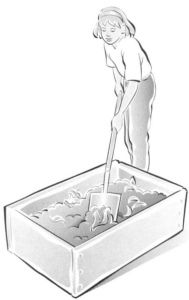

5. a. Make a sketch of a 1-3-5 box. Label the edges of the box.

b. Sketch three boxes that have twice the volume of a 1-3-5 box. Label each box with its dimensions.

6. a. Make scale drawings of three cubes: one with edges measuring 1 ft, one with edges measuring 2 ft, and one with edges measuring 3 ft. For each cube, tell what length in the drawing represents 1 ft. In other words, give the scale for each drawing.

b. Find the volume of each cube in part a.

c. Find the surface area of each cube in part a.

d. Describe what happens to the volume of a cube when the edge lengths are doubled, tripled, quadrupled, and so on.

e. Describe what happens to the surface area of a cube when the edge lengths are doubled, tripled, quadrupled, and so on.

7. For every ton of paper that is recycled, about 17 trees and 3.3 yd^3 of landfill space are saved. In the United States, 500,000 trees are used each week to produce the Sunday papers. If one Sunday, all the newspapers were made from 100% recycled paper, how much landfill would be saved?

8. In the United States, an average of 2.7 pounds of garbage per person is delivered to available landfills each day. A cubic foot of compressed garbage weighs about 50 pounds.

a. Estimate the amount of landfill used by a family of four in one year.

b. Estimate the amount of landfill used by the families of all your classmates in one year. Assume each family has four people.

9. Each year the United States generates about 450 million cubic yards of solid waste. Mr. Costello's classroom is 42 ft long, 30 ft wide, and 12 ft high. How many rooms of this size would be needed to hold all this garbage?

Connections

10. Mary's class decides to build a cylindrical compost box. Mary calculates that a cylindrical container with a height of 2 ft and a radius of 1 ft would decompose 0.5 pound of garbage each day. She calls this container a *1-2 cylinder*.

    a. How does the volume of the 1-2 cylinder compare to the volume of the 1-2-3 box?

    b. How does the surface area of the 1-2 cylinder compare to the surface area of the 1-2-3 box?

    c. Mary's class estimates that they throw away about 1 pound of organic waste at school each day. What size cylinder should they build to handle this much waste?

11. At the movie theater, Ted is trying to decide whether to buy a large popcorn or two small popcorns. Both sizes come in cylindrical containers. Ted thinks that the heights of the containers are about the same and that the radius of the large container is about twice the radius of the small container. A large popcorn costs $3.00, and a small popcorn costs $1.50. To get the most popcorn for his $3.00, should Ted buy one large popcorn or two small popcorns? Explain your answer.

12. The Whole Earth Compost Company builds and sells 1-2-3 compost boxes. They need to store a supply of the boxes in their warehouse to fill customers' orders. The sketch below shows a 1-2-3 box and the space in the warehouse allotted for the boxes.

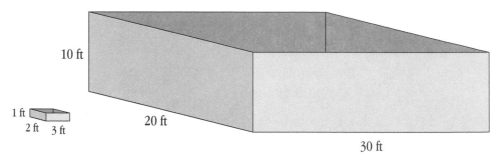

a. How many 1-2-3 boxes could be stored in one layer on the floor of the storage space?

b. How many layers of boxes could be stacked in the storage space?

c. How many boxes could be stored in the storage space?

In 13–15, find the volume and surface area of the box.

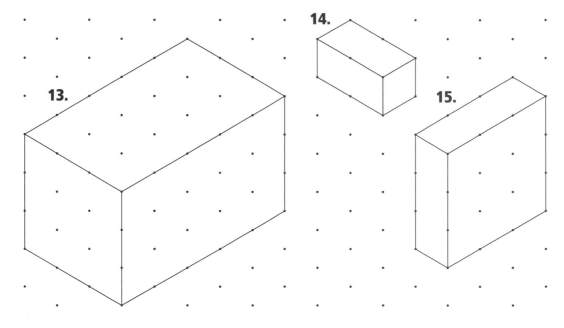

Extensions

16. Is the price of cereal directly related to the volume of the box? Collect some data to help you answer this question.

    a. Record the dimensions and prices of two or three different size boxes of the same cereal brand.

    b. Calculate the volume of each box.

    c. Calculate the cost per unit of volume for each box. Compare the results for the different boxes.

    d. Write a short report summarizing what you learned about the relationship between box size and cereal price.

17. The following sketch shows a "tilted box" in which the base, top, and smaller sides are rectangles, and the other two faces are non-rectangular parallelograms.

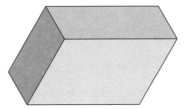

    a. What measurements would you need to find the volume of this box? How would you use these measurements to calculate the volume?

    b. What measurements would you need to find the surface area of this box? How would you use these measurements to calculate the surface area?

18. Think about a "sliceable" rectangular prism, such as a cake, a loaf of bread, or a brick of cheese.

    a. How many different ways can you slice such a prism into two pieces of equal volume?

    b. If the prism were a cube, how many ways could you slice it into two pieces of equal volume?

19. The dimensions of cylinder A are twice the dimensions of cylinder B.

    a. What is the ratio of the radius of cylinder A to the radius of cylinder B?

    b. What is the ratio of the height of cylinder A to the height of cylinder B?

    c. What is the ratio of the surface area of cylinder A to the surface area of cylinder B?

    d. What is the ratio of the volume of cylinder A to the volume of cylinder B?

20. The dimensions of cylinder A are three times the dimensions of cylinder B. Repeat parts a–d of question 19 for these cylinders.

21. The dimensions of cylinder A are four times the dimensions of cylinder B. Repeat parts a–d of question 19 for these cylinders.

22. Natasha built a model cruise ship from a kit. She was trying to imagine what the actual cruise ship would look like. The scale factor from the model ship to the actual ship is 200.

    a. If the length of the model ship is 25 cm, what is the length of the actual ship?

    b. If the cold-storage space of the model has a capacity of 600 cm^3, what is the capacity of the cold-storage space of the actual ship?

    c. The area of the dance floor on the actual cruise ship is 250 m^2. What is the area of the dance floor on the model?

    d. The cylindrical smokestack on the model has a height of 4 cm and a radius of 1.5 cm.

        i. What are the dimensions of the smokestack on the actual ship?

        ii. What is the volume of the smokestack on the actual ship?

        iii. What is the surface area of the smokestack on the actual ship?

Mathematical Reflections

In this investigation, you learned how changing the dimensions of a rectangular box affects its volume and how changing the volume of a rectangular box affects its dimensions. These questions will help you summarize what you have learned:

1 Suppose you wanted to build a rectangular box with twice the volume of a given rectangular box. How could you determine the possible dimensions for the new box?

2 Describe how the volume and surface area of a rectangular prism change as each of its dimensions is doubled, tripled, quadrupled, and so on.

Think about your answers to these questions, discuss your ideas with other students and your teacher, and then write a summary of your findings in your journal.

Finding Volumes of Irregular Objects

You have solved many problems in which you had to calculate the volume or surface area of a prism, a cylinder, a cone, or a sphere. However, many three-dimensional objects do not have such regular shapes. In this investigation, you will explore finding volumes of odd-shaped, or irregular, objects.

7.1 Displacing Water

According to legend, Archimedes, a Greek scientist in the third century B.C., made an important discovery while taking a bath. He noticed that the water level rose when he sat down in the tub. He figured out that he could calculate the volume of his body—or any other object—by submerging it in water and finding the difference between the combined volume of the water and the object, and the volume of the water alone. This difference in volumes is called *water displacement.* It is said that Archimedes was so excited about his discovery that he jumped from his bath and, without dressing, ran into the streets shouting "Eureka!"

Think about this!

Does Archimedes' discovery suggest a way to measure the volume of an irregular shape?

In this problem, you measure the volume of water in *milliliters,* a unit commonly used to express the volume of liquids. As part of the problem, you will figure out how to convert milliliters to cubic centimeters.

Problem 7.1

You will need a measuring box or cylinder with milliliter markings, water, a few centimeter cubes, and some odd-shaped objects like stones.

Fill the measuring container about halfway with water. Record the volume of the water in milliliters.

To find the volume of an object, drop it into the container and find the volume of water that is displaced. That is, find the difference between the combined volume of the water and the object, and the volume of the water alone.

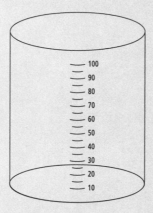

A. How much water is displaced when you drop a centimeter cube into the container? What does this tell you about the relationship between one milliliter and one cubic centimeter?

B. Use this method to find the volume in cubic centimeters of some odd-shaped objects.

Problem 7.1 Follow-Up

Give examples of objects whose volume cannot be measured by this method. Explain why this method would not work.

As you work on these ACE questions, use your calculator whenever you need it.

Applications

1. A cylinder with a diameter of 5 cm contains some water. Five identical marbles are dropped into the cylinder, and the water level rises by 1 cm. What is the volume of one marble?

2. A rectangular 1-2-3 box is half full of water.

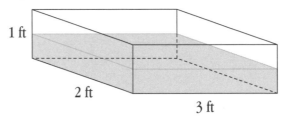

1 ft

2 ft

3 ft

 a. What is the total volume of the box?

 b. What is the water level in the box?

 c. Several large stones are dropped into the box, and the water level rises to $\frac{3}{4}$ full. What is the total volume of the stones?

3. A gallon of paint covers about 400 ft^2 of surface area. When an artist painted a statue he had carved, he used about 0.25 gallon of paint. What is the approximate surface area of the statue?

4. A rectangular juice box contains 250 milliliters of juice. Give the dimensions of a box that will hold this amount of juice.

5. An average adult has a mass of about 78 kilograms and a surface area of about 9675 cm^2. A film of water about 0.05 cm thick clings to our skin when we step out of the bath.

 a. What volume of water clings to an average adult when he steps out of the bath?

 b. If 1 cm^3 of water has a mass of 1 gram, what percent of an average adult's body mass is the mass of the water that clings to him after a shower?

Extensions

6. Paper often comes in packages of 500 sheets, called reams. A particular ream of paper has a length of 28 cm, a width of 21.5 cm, and a height of 5.5 cm.

    a. What is the volume of a sheet of paper?

    b. What is the thickness of a sheet of paper?

7. A particular iceberg is shaped like a mountain with a height of 1250 m above the water level and a distance of 132 km around the base (1 km = 1000 m) at water level.

    a. What shape most closely resembles the top of a mountain?

    b. Estimate the volume of the part of the iceberg that is above water level.

Mathematical Reflections

In this investigation, you found volumes of odd-shaped objects by measuring water displacement. These questions will help you summarize what you have learned:

1 Describe how you can find the volume of an odd-shaped object by measuring water displacement, and give an example of a situation in which this method would be useful.

2 What is the relationship between cubic centimeters and milliliters? How can you prove this relationship?

Think about your answers to these questions, discuss your ideas with other students and your teacher, and then write a summary of your findings in your journal.

Package Design Contest

The Worldwide Sporting Company wants new package designs for its table-tennis balls (Ping-Pong balls). The company's table-tennis balls are about 3.8 cm in diameter. There are three main requirements for the packages:

- The board of directors wants to have three different size packages: small, medium, and large.
- The president of the company wants the cost of the packages to be a primary consideration.
- The sales manager wants the packages to be appealing to customers, to stack easily, and to look good on store shelves.

The company holds a package design contest, and you decide to enter.

- You must design three different packages for the table-tennis balls.
- You must submit your designs and a written proposal to WSC.
- You must try, in your written proposal, to convince WSC to use your designs.

Include the following things in your proposal:

1. A description of the shape or shapes of the packages and an explanation for why you selected these shapes.

2. Patterns for each package that, when they are cut out, folded, and taped together, will make models of your packages. Use centimeter grid paper to make your patterns.

3. Cost estimates to construct your designs. The packaging material costs $0.005 per square centimeter.

4. An explanation of how you have addressed WSC's requirements.

Remember, you are trying to convince WSC that your designs are the best and that they meet the requirements. Your written proposal should be neat, well organized, and easy to read so that the company officials can follow your work and ideas easily.

Unit Reflections

While working on the problems in this unit you developed strategies for finding *surface area*, *volume*, and *flat patterns* for rectangular prisms and cylinders. You used the relationships of other figures to cylinders to find the volume of shapes such as *cones* and *spheres,* and irregular solids. Finally, you discovered the effects of enlargement and reduction on dimensions, surface area, and volume of prisms.

Using Your Understanding of Volume and Surface Area—To test your understanding of volume and surface area, consider the following problems that require knowledge and skills you developed during the investigations of this unit.

1 *The drawing on the right is a flat pattern for a rectangular prism.*

a. What are the dimensions of the box that can be made from the flat pattern?

b. What is the surface area of the box?

c. What is the volume of the box?

d. Draw two other flat patterns that will produce boxes of the same size and shape.

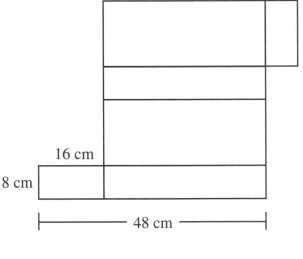

16 cm

16 cm

8 cm

48 cm

2 Sweet-Tooth Chocolates is marketing a special assortment of caramels. They want to put the 40 individual caramels into a rectangular box. Each caramel is a 1-inch cube. The caramels should completely fill the box.

   a. Which arrangement of caramels would require the most cardboard for a box?

   b. Which arrangement of caramels would require the least cardboard?

   c. Make sketches of the boxes you described in part a and part b and label the dimensions.

   d. Draw flat plans for each box and add the minimum number of flaps needed to fold and then glue the pattern together so that the top opens.

   e. If each dimension of the box in part b is doubled, how many more caramels could be packaged in the new box?

3 The Just-Add-Water Company has decided to change the packaging for a breakfast drink, Twang. Twang used to come in cylindrical containers with a base diameter of 6 inches and a height of 10 inches. The new container will be a square prism as shown in this sketch.

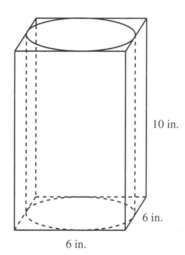

10 in.

6 in.

6 in.

   a. What is the volume of the original cylindrical container?

   b. How much more juice can the rectangular prism hold than the cylindrical container?

   c. Suppose that the cost per cubic inch of Twang is to be the same for both containers. How much should a new box of Twang cost if the original container cost $2.19?

   d. The company is also considering selling the drink in a cone with the same volume as the cylinder. Describe possible dimensions for such a cone.

Explaining Your Reasoning—To answer problems about surface area and volume of solid figures you have to know the meaning of those terms and some strategies for calculating the measurements from given dimensions of various figures.

1. What do *volume* and *surface area* measurements tell about a solid figure?

2. What algebraic formulas will show how to calculate surface area, A, and volume, V, of the figures drawn here?

a. a rectangular prism

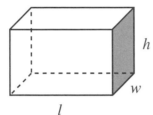

b. a cylinder

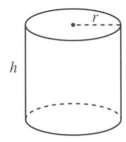

3. How would you convince someone that the formulas given in Question 2 are correct?

4. How are the volumes of cylinders, cones, and spheres related?

5. If you know the volume of an object such as a box, a cylinder, or a cone, can you determine its surface area? If you know the surface area, can you find the volume?

6. How are the surface areas and volumes of similar solid figures related?

Measurement of surface area and volume for solid figures is used in many practical, scientific, and engineering problems. You will encounter the key ideas about area and volume in many future *Connected Mathematics* units, in other mathematics subjects such as geometry and calculus, and in many situations of daily life such as packing, storing and building tasks.

base The bottom face of a three-dimensional shape.

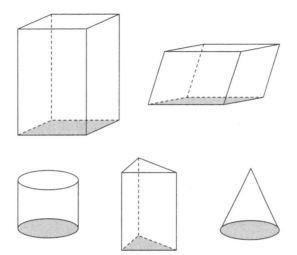

cone A three-dimensional shape with a circular end and a pointed end.

cube A three-dimensional shape with six identical square faces.

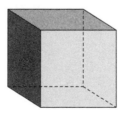

cylinder A three-dimensional shape with two opposite faces that are congruent circles. A rectangle (the lateral surface) is "wrapped around" the circular ends.

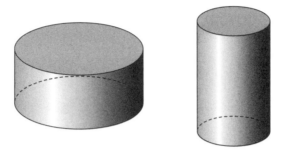

edge The line segment formed where two faces of a three-dimensional shape meet.

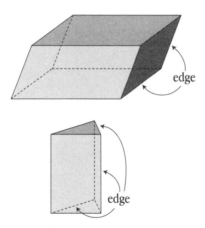

face A polygon that forms one of the flat surfaces of a three-dimensional shape.

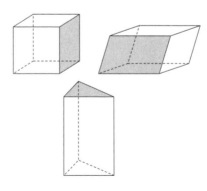

flat pattern An arrangement of attached polygons that can be folded into a three-dimensional shape.

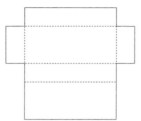

oblique prism A prism whose vertical faces are not all rectangles.

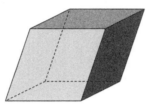

prism A three-dimensional shape with a top and bottom that are congruent polygons and faces that are parallelograms.

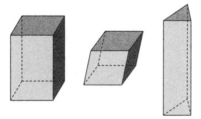

rectangular prism A prism with a top and bottom that are congruent rectangles.

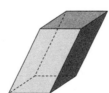

Right rectangular prism   Oblique rectangular prism

right prism A prism whose vertical faces are rectangles.

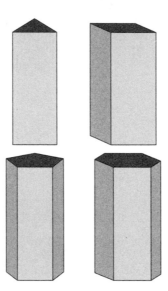

sphere A three-dimensional shape whose surface consists of all the points that are a given distance from the center of the shape.

surface area The area required to cover a three-dimensional shape. In a prism, it is the sum of the areas of all the faces.

unit cube A cube whose edges are 1 unit long. It is the basic unit of measurement for volume.

volume The amount of space occupied by, or the capacity of, a three-dimensional shape. It is the number of unit cubes that will fit into a three-dimensional shape.

área de la superficie El área requerida para cubrir una figura tridimensional. En un prisma, es la suma de las áreas de todas las caras.

arista El segmento de recta formado donde se encuentran dos caras de una figura tridimensional.

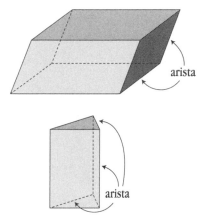

base La cara inferior de una figura tridimensional.

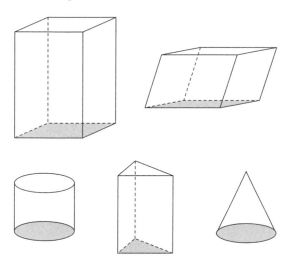

cara Un polígono que forma una de las superficies planas de una figura tridimensional.

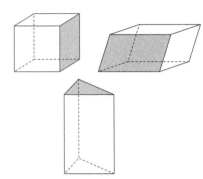

cilindro Una figura tridimensional con dos caras opuestas que son círculos congruentes. Un rectángulo (la cara lateral) está "envuelto alrededor de" los extremos circulares.

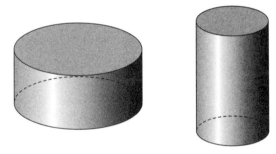

cono Una figura tridimensional con un extremo circular y un extremo en punta.

cubo Una figura tridimensional con seis caras cuadradas idénticas.

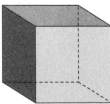

esfera Una figura tridimensional cuya superficie consiste en todos los puntos ubicados a una distancia dada del centro de la figura.

patrón plano Una disposición de polígonos contiguos que puede plegarse de modo de formar una figura tridimensional.

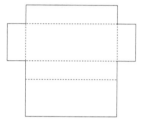

prisma Una figura tridimensional cuya parte superior y cuyo fondo son polígonos congruentes y cuyas caras son paralelogramos.

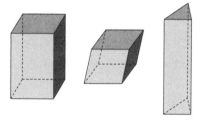

prisma oblicuo Un prisma cuyas caras verticales no son todas rectángulos.

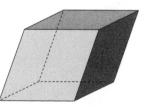

prisma rectangular Un prisma cuya parte superior y cuyo fondo son rectángulos congruentes.

Prisma
rectangular
recto

Prisma
rectangular
oblicuo

prisma recto Un prisma cuyas caras verticales son rectángulos.

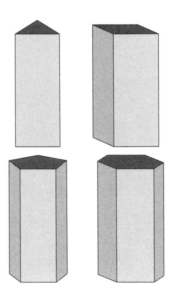

unidad cúbica Un cubo cuyas aristas miden 1 unidad de longitud. Es la unidad básica de medición para el volumen.

volumen La cantidad de espacio ocupado por una figura tridimensional o la capacidad de dicha figura. Es el número de unidades cúbicas que cabrán en una figura tridimensional.

Index